Don't Fall for Deception: Spotting and Escaping Romance Scams

- A Definitive Step-by-Step Handbook

Harrell Howard

Chapter 1: Introduction to Romance Scams

Romance scams, also known as confidence scams or catfishing, are a type of online fraud where criminals create fake online identities and form relationships with victims to manipulate them into sending money. These scammers prey on people looking for love and companionship online, gaining their trust over weeks or months before asking for financial help and then disappearing with their money.

According to the FBI, romance scams cost victims more than $600 million in 2021 alone. The number of reported romance scams has been steadily rising over the past several years as more people turn to online dating apps and websites to find relationships. However, many people are unaware of how prevalent these scams are and how to recognize the warning signs.

This definitive handbook will provide readers with extensive information on how to spot romance scams and protect themselves from being manipulated and deceived. It covers topics such as:

- The psychological tricks used by scammers to build rapport and gain trust
- Common tactics and scenarios used in romance scams
- Red flags to watch out for when getting to know someone online
- Safety precautions to take while online dating
- Steps to take if you suspect you are being scammed
- How to report romance scams and warn others
- Support resources for victims of these scams

By learning about the deceptive techniques used in romance scams, readers will be equipped with the knowledge needed to avoid being taken advantage of. This handbook aims to spread awareness about this issue and prevent more innocent victims from having their hearts broken and bank accounts drained by these criminal scammers.

Chapter 2: Understanding the Psychology Behind Romance Scams

Romance scammers are masters of manipulation and deception. They utilize sophisticated psychological tactics to take advantage of people seeking love and companionship online. Understanding how scammers think and operate is key to spotting and avoiding romance scams.

This chapter will dive into the psychology behind romance scams and what drives scammers to heartlessly target and exploit people in this way.

Human Emotional Needs - Scammers recognize and aim to fulfill basic human emotional needs such as love, belonging, and connection. By pretending to be a loving romantic partner, they fulfill these unmet needs in their victims, building strong bonds and trust.

Grooming - Scammers spend weeks or months grooming targets through romantic gestures and constant communication. This makes the victim feel dependent on the relationship.

Trauma Bonding - Scammers will often combine affection with pleas for financial help, creating a trauma bond. The victim feels they need to support their partner.

Suspension of Disbelief - Targets get so swept up in the romance they ignore red flags. People tend to believe what they want to believe when strong emotions are involved.

Sunk Cost Fallacy - The more time, money, and emotion someone invests in a relationship, the harder it becomes to cut losses and leave. Scammers leverage this to keep victims on the hook.

Cognitive Dissonance - When scam victims are confronted with evidence they're being exploited, it creates intense mental discomfort. Easier to rationalize away the proof than accept the horrible truth.

Isolation - Scammers recommend moving communications off dating sites quickly and discourage victims from discussing the relationship with friends or family who might detect the scam. This isolates the victim.

Scarcity & Urgency - Scammers create a sense of urgency and scarcity around money requests, jobs, or other issues to bypass critical thinking. Saying no or asking questions becomes unthinkable.

Understanding these psychological drivers helps shed light on how even smart, emotionally balanced people can fall victim to expert manipulators. It also equips people to detect red-flag behaviors.

Chapter 3: Warning Signs of a Romance Scam

Romance scammers have playbooks they closely follow when interacting with and grooming victims. While they are masters of manipulation, their tactics and behaviors tend to follow some common patterns that can serve as important red flags. Here are the top warning signs to recognize when getting to know someone online:

- They quickly profess strong feelings of love - scammers will often tell you they love you within days or weeks before really getting to know you. Genuine romantic interest takes time to develop.

- They are traveling or live overseas - scammers claim to be abroad for work, military service, or personal reasons to justify never meeting in person and needing money wired.

- They have an elaborate sob story
- scammers will share tales of
personal tragedy, family deaths,
injuries, legal troubles, or other
misfortunes to gain sympathy and
financial assistance.

- Their profile seems too perfect -
scammers create idealized profiles
using stolen photos of attractive
models, lists of high-paying
careers, and exaggerated personal
details. Too good to be true.

- Inconsistencies in their story -
since the details are fabricated,
scammers have a hard time
keeping facts straight over long
interactions. Spot conflicting
details.

- Quickly trying to move off the
dating site - scammers will push to
continue communications via
email, messaging apps, phone, etc
where there is less monitoring and
accountability.

- They avoid video chatting -
scammers will make excuses as to

why they can't video chat to avoid revealing they are impersonating someone.

- They ask probing personal questions - scammers will fish for details they can leverage like income, assets, place of work, etc. Deflect answering.

- They have financial troubles - scammers will eventually ask for money to deal with claimed financial issues or support a business opportunity.

- They want financial help leaving the country - a common scam is needing cash to book a flight or pay a visa fee to finally come meet you after months apart.

- Refusing to meet in person - even if they live locally, scammers will avoid meeting claiming they are out of town, have an injury, sick relative etc.

Being aware of these common patterns and behaviors can help identifying and avoiding scammers

who are looking to take advantage
of kind-hearted singles seeking
love. Listen to your instincts - if it
looks too good to be genuine, it
probably is. Proceed with caution.

Chapter 4: Common Tactics Used By Romance Scammers

Romance scammers employ a variety of manipulative tactics and scenarios when targeting victims. Being familiar with their common ploys and routines can help raise red flags early in an interaction before the scam fully develops. Here are some of the favorite tricks and techniques used by scammers:

Military Personnel - They claim to be deployed overseas with the military to justify delays meeting in person and the need to communicate online. Asking for money to buy leave time to visit is common.

Foreign Business Owner - They say they are working abroad to set up lucrative overseas business opportunities. Need investment funds from the victim to get it going and share in profits.

Stranded Traveler - They claim they came to the victim's country but then had an emergency like a mugging or passport theft. Now they need money for food, lodging and to get new documents.

Medical Emergencies - They describe health crises such as car crashes, rare illnesses or injuries to loved ones, asking the victim to help cover medical costs.

Legal Troubles - Scammers spin tales of legal woes like customs problems, visa issues, lawsuits, arrests etc. and ask the victim to wire bail money or lawyer fees.

Unexpected Windfall - After trust is built, the scammer shares exciting news of an upcoming business payout, inheritance, lottery win etc. and promises to use it to visit the victim. They just need a little bit of money to receive the full amount.

Falling in Love Quickly - Scammers rapidly profess love and make elaborate romantic promises to hook the victim's emotions and rapidly move into exploiting them for money before thinking critically.

Leveraging Faith - Scammers research the backgrounds of victims and adapt their persona and stories to leverage faith, church, and spiritual beliefs if the target is religious. This builds false trust.

Understanding the common scenarios and sob stories used lets potential victims analyze interactions more objectively. When a new online match aligns with these known stories, it should provoke greater scrutiny and verification before believing or sending money.

Chapter 5: How to Protect Yourself from Romance Scams

While romance scammers can be incredibly convincing online, there are steps individuals can take to greatly reduce the chances of being victimized. Here are proactive measures for protecting yourself while dating online:

1. Never send money - Money requests should be an immediate red flag. Never transfer funds for someone you haven't met, no matter how convincing their story. Genuine partners will not ask this early on.

2. Do reverse image searches - Take profile pictures and do a reverse image search using Google, Bing, etc. Stolen photos used by scammers may show up linking them to other online profiles.

3. Video chat before growing attached - Don't deeply invest in the relationship until you have

dates over video to confirm their identity and details. Avoided or staged video chats are a warning sign.

4. Look for inconsistent details - Review your chats for inconsistent facts about their location, career, family etc. Scammers struggle to remember lies.

5. Stay on the dating site /app - Don't quickly transition to email or messenger where there are less protections. Keep early interactions on the dating platform

Chapter 6: Step-by-Step Guide to Spotting and Escaping Romance Scams

If you suspect the new romantic interest you met online may be trying to scam you, there are concrete steps you can take to detect and get out of the fraudulent relationship safely. Here is an actionable guide:

1. Document all communications - Save chat logs, emails, texts etc. to have a record of interactions. This evidence will be critical if reporting the scammer later.

2. Fact check their claims - Reverse search profile images, run background checks on names/numbers, and verify factual details through public records. See if their story checks out.

3. Call out inconsistencies - Note any suspicious changes in their story over time. Directly but non-confrontationally ask for

clarification on contradictions you've identified.

4. Ask to meet in person - Insist on a local first date. A continued stream of excuses is a major red flag.

5. Involve friends or family - Don't keep the relationship secret due to "scammer's" wishes. Get other perspectives from loved ones you trust.

6. Slow down - Cease all talk of future plans, emotional intimacy, and any money transfers. Evaluate with logic.

7. Cut contact - If evidence confirms a romance scam, immediately block the individual on all channels. Cut all contact harshly.

8. Seek emotional support - Confide in loved ones, counselors, or support groups. Do not feel ashamed—these scammers are experts in exploitation.

9. Report the scammer - Notify the dating site/app, cybercrime divisions of law enforcement, banks, and organizations like the FTC. Prevent others from being victimized.

10. Be vigilant moving forward - Use the lessons learned to keep an eye out for red flags when exploring future online relationships. Don't become jaded—there are sincere people out there too.

Following these steps at the first signs, something is amiss can help targets of romance scams determine if they are being taken advantage of and exit the unhealthy relationship.

Chapter 7: Reporting Romance Scams to the Authorities

A critical aspect of stopping romance scammers and their abuse is reporting them to the relevant authorities and watchdog organizations. Doing so creates official records on the scammers, helps identify and stop them, and prevents further innocent victims. Here are key places to report suspected romance scams:

- Dating Site or App - Notify the dating platform where you initially met the scammer. They can ban fraudulent accounts and use details to screen for the same scammer under different profiles.

- Local Police - File reports about the scam with your local police department. They may conduct broader investigations if more victims surface.

- FBI IC3 - The FBI's Internet Crime Complaint Center (IC3)

compiles internet scam reports in a central database accessible to law enforcement.

- FTC - The Federal Trade Commission's reporting system aggregates scam information helpful for investigating and prosecuting large-scale or repeat offender scams.

- FraudAlert.org - This non-profit organization works with agencies globally to track and shutdown romance scam operations by region.

- Nigerian EFCC - The Nigerian Economic and Financial Crimes Commission investigates many romance scam rings originating abroad.

- Money Transfer Services - Notify companies like Western Union or MoneyGram with details on fraudulent transactions. They can attempt recovering funds.

- Banks - Report any fraudulent use of bank accounts associated with the scam, like deposits or transfers. Accounts can be frozen and limited.

- Social Media Networks - Report fake accounts on platforms like Facebook, Instagram, Google, etc. to try getting them taken down.

Romance scam victims shouldn't feel ashamed or hide the fact they've been exploited. Reporting the scams helps prevent continued harm and makes it riskier for the criminals. Agencies also may be able to recover some lost money.

Chapter 8: Support Resources for Victims of Romance Scams

Being deceived and betrayed by a romance scammer can be emotionally devastating and financially ruinous. Know that there are many support resources available to help guide and comfort victims through the aftermath. Here are places to turn to for assistance:

- Local Counselors or Therapists - Seek licensed mental health professionals who specialize in recovering from deception and manipulation. Many victims struggle with trust issues afterwards.

- Support Groups - Organizations like RomanceScam.org host online group meetings where victims can share stories, advice, and encouragement in a judgement-free zone.

- Adult Protective Services - APS agencies provide guidance on getting finances in order, accessing government benefits, and managing affairs after financial abuse of elderly or disabled individuals.

- Legal Assistance - Seek attorneys skilled in cases of online impersonation, fraud, or exploitation for help determining options to recover some monetary damages. Pro bono lawyers may be available.

- Case Managers - Social workers can act as case managers by touching base regularly, connecting victims to resources, and checking on their mental health status during recovery.

- Family and Friends - Don't isolate. Surround yourself with a strong support network of loved ones you can be open and vulnerable with following the betrayal.

- Self-Care Routines - Recovery takes time. Establish practical self-care routines focused on improving sleep, diet, exercise, social connections, and mindfulness skills.

- Online Recovery Forums - Anonymously read stories of others who survived romance scams and join discussions threads to know you aren't alone.

There is no shame in admitting an elaborate deception. Focus recovery efforts on processing the trauma, limiting financial damages, and restoring a sense of optimism and trust over time. Support is available.

Chapter 9: Real-Life Stories of Individuals Who Fell Victim to Romance Scams

To truly understand the devastating emotional and financial toll that romance scams inflict, it's helpful to look at real-world cases of individuals who were victimized by these expert manipulators. Here are some true stories:

Jennifer's Story:

Jennifer was a retired widow who lost $400,000 in life savings to an overseas man she met on a dating site who strung her along for over a year claiming he was coming to be with her. He made endless excuses and asked for money to deal with claimed travel complications. By the time she realized it was all a ruse, it was too late. She lost nearly everything but is slowly rebuilding with the support of loved ones.

Tom's Story:

Tom was going through a divorce when he matched an attractive younger woman on Tinder who said she was stranded after losing her wallet on a trip to meet him. Over two months, he wired her $5,000 to pay for food and lodging under the pretense they'd be repaid once she got home. It was only after speaking to his son that he realized the increasingly elaborate stories were completely fabricated to exploit his desire for companionship.

Olivia's Story:

Olivia reconnected online with a childhood best friend who said he needed to take over his sick father's business dealings in Ghana. Over months, she sent $15,000 that he promised to repay once he secured overseas deals. After not hearing from him for weeks, Olivia eventually accepted she'd been cruelly tricked by someone exploiting nostalgia.

Maria's Story:

Maria started chatting with a man on a dating site who said he was being sent to serve overseas in the military. They spoke for months developing a deep connection before he began asking for money for various needs related to his service. In total Maria lost $60,000 over 2 years before finally realizing he was not who he said he was, and that she'd been used in an elaborate deception preying on her patriotism.

These real-life examples underscore the deep emotional pain and financial consequences that romance scam victims experience. By learning how to identify red flags earlier on, the financial and emotional costs can be minimized.

Chapter 10: Conclusion and Final Thoughts

Romance scams can ruin lives. The criminals running these fraudulent schemes specialize in single-mindedly manipulating human emotion for their own gain with no regard for the trauma inflicted on their victims. However, by learning common tactics these scammers use, individuals can equip themselves to detect red flags early and avoid being exploited.

When exploring any new online relationship, proceed carefully and rationally. Do extensive vetting, fact checking, and gradual trust building before investing your emotions or finances. Follow protocols like insisting on video chats, looking for inconsistent details, and involving friends for outside perspectives.

If you do suspect you are being scammed, immediately cease all contact and money transfers.

Gather evidence, report the scammer to every relevant authority, and lean on your support systems while healing. By remaining vigilant and protecting your heart, you can find genuine love - even in the digital world filled with risks and deception. Stay encouraged.

With awareness, education, and some practical precautions, everyone can more safely find meaningful connections online. Don't become jaded or bitter. Millions of authentic relationships continue to form through online platforms. By staying informed and alert, you can spot and stop scammers in their tracks and hopefully prevent other trusting individuals from being victimized.

ABOUT THE AUTHOR

Harrell Howard is a versatile author with a passion for writing on technology, fiction, kids' books, and money matters. His work encompasses thought-provoking technology articles, enchanting fiction tales, captivating children's books, and insightful money-related pieces. With a commitment to research and a knack for storytelling, Harrell's writing resonates with readers of all ages, leaving a lasting impact on the literary world.